Dear friend,
Here's the thing—your Mom and Dad and family love you a lot. Even Buddy Bablu loves you a lot—though you don't know him yet. (You will meet him in the story—keep reading!) And because they love you, they want you to be safe. But, life is grand! So they also want you to enjoy it, be brave, and have many wonderful adventures.

So, try things! Explore, fall down, try again. Just make sure that along the way you are being safe. We all love you!

And now, presenting ... The Sensational Safety Puppet Show!

Truly,
Kimmie Auntie

PAPUUUUU!

Come See the Sensational Safety Puppet Show!

by
Kimmie Auntie

Illustrations by
Ayeshe Sadr & Ishaan Dasgupta

another title brought to you from
the BEST ME series

SCHOLASTIC
New York Toronto London Auckland
Sydney New Delhi Hong Kong

For Miss Vids, our delightful diva with her sweet soul and my Mom, who writes oodles of entertaining puppet shows

Published by Scholastic India Pvt. Ltd.
A subsidiary of Scholastic Inc., New York, 10012 (USA).
Publishers since 1920, with international operations in Canada, Australia, New Zealand, the United Kingdom, India, and Hong Kong.

For information regarding permission, write to:
Scholastic India Pvt. Ltd.
A-27, Ground Floor, Sigma Centre
Infocity-1, Sector 34, Gurgaon 122001 (India)

This edition: October 2022

ISBN-13: 978-93-8610-674-2

Printed in India at Sterling Graphics Pvt. Ltd., Manesar

Vidya came howling at a full run, right into Papu's lap.
He smoothed her wild curls, "Beti! What is wrong?"

Gulping tears, she blurted, "PAPU—
Shlok broke his arm. He's in the hospital!"

Papu cuddled Vidya to comfort her.

"Papu, I don't want my friends to get hurt! How can I help them be safe?"

"What do **YOU** think you could do, Vidya?" Papu asked. He knew she was a smart girl.

Vidya brightened, "Let's put on a safety puppet show for Shlok and invite my class! We will cheer him up—and everyone will learn how to be safe!"

"Wonderful idea, Vidya! I'll help you."

Vidya cut fabric, glued little clothes, and drew itty-bitty faces. Papu hung a scrap of red velvet for a curtain.

Dancing a puppet around, Vidya beamed, "Yup! This is going to work!"

Puppet Show

The next day in Shlok's hospital room, the children tromped in and sat in wiggly rows. When they saw the red velvet curtain, their eyes grew big.

Giggling and whispering, they wondered what a safety puppet show would be. Shlok was the most curious of all.

Seeing all of her friends, Vidya swallowed nervously. "Papu..."

Papu kissed her head, "You can do it, Vidya!" She took a deep breath.

WELCOME
SENSATI
Let the

to the SAFETY
...NAL PUPPET SHOW
SHOW BEGIIIIN!

Papu pulled open the curtain with a drumroll...

drdrdrdrrrrrrrum!

"STICK WITH US AND LEARN TO STAY SAFE!"

sang out the puppets. (Puppets love to sing.)

Now all the children were quiet and only wiggling a wee bit.

"Hallooo! I'M BUDDY BABLU!"
Prancing forward, he sang,

"I never go off by myself.
I always take a friend.
You should too—
follow the buddy rule!"

"NOW INTRODUCING MY FRIEND,
MISS MATCHES MIRA!"

Mira sang,
"I never play with fire matches.
I take them to my Mom.
You should too—
follow the matches rule."

“NEXT UP IS
RAILWAY RANI!”

“I never jump on railway tracks.
I walk on the platform.
You should too—
follow the railway rule!”

“LAST UP IS
SEATBELT SAAM!!”

“I don't hop around in the car.
I will click my seatbelt.
You should too—
follow the seatbelt rule.”

Vidya used her best announcer voice.

"THANK YOU FOR THE TIPS, SAFETY PUPPETS! BUT CHILDREN— CAN YOU HELP US ALL STAY SAFE TOO?"

The children turned and looked at each other. Could they do it?

One by one, the children chimed in...
I make sure I can always see my Mom or Dad when I'm playing at the park.
I'll take care when I jump!
I always take my medicine properly!

I don't stick anything in the electric socket.
If someone tried to take me away, I would scream and yell and kick hard!
I don't ride my bike in the road. And I look both ways before I cross the street!

Buddy Bablu cheered, "You got it! Now give me a high-five and promise to stay safe!"

Shlok slid out of bed and high-fived the puppet, "I'll do it, Buddy Bablu!" All the other children followed him.

And the Safety Puppets took a bow.

THE END

Discussion Questions for Parents and Teachers:

What does it mean to be safe?

Why is this important? Why do we care if you are safe? If a parent insists you be safe, does that mean the parent isn't nice?

How can we practice _____ safety? (Pick something your child needs to specifically work on.)

Activities:

1. Make one of the Safety Puppets with your kids. If your child needs a different lesson than those in the story, feel free to improvise and create a new Safety Puppet. Copy the invitation from the book and perform your safety show for other members of the family or perhaps the child's class.

2. Choose a song that your child knows and have them practice singing the music by reciting your cell phone number and address. Twinkle Twinkle Little Star is an easy one to use.

3. Be sure to explain to your child why safety matters. You just want them to be safe! You are not mean to insist they follow safety rules such as a seat belt. Discuss each safety rule in the story and be sure your child is clear.

*Parenting Tip: Model good behaviour. Wear a motorcycle helmet, wear a seat belt and don't talk on the cell phone while driving, look both ways as you cross streets.